MACMILLAN WRITER'S PRIZ

Daudi's Dream

Susan Mugizi Kajura

Macmillan Education
Between Towns Road, Oxford, OX4 3PP
A division of Macmillan Publishers Limited
Companies and representatives throughout the world

www.macmillan-africa.com

ISBN 0 333 99248 2

Text © Susan Mugizi Kajura 2002
Design and illustration © Macmillan Publishers Limited 2002

First published 2002

All rights reserved: no part of this publication may be reproduced, stored in a retrieval system, transmitted in any form or by any means, electronic, mechanical, photocopying, recording, or otherwise, without the prior written permission of the publishers.

Designed by Charles Design Associates, Southampton
Illustrated by Sally Linton
Cover design by Gary Fielder at AC Design
Cover illustration by Sally Linton

Printed and bound in Malaysia

2006 2005 2004 2003 2002
10 9 8 7 6 5 4 3 2 1

1	In the quarry	5
2	Daudi gets a job	11
3	A lucky break	16
4	The bottle opener	21
5	The big day	26

1 In the quarry

Down in the quarry, Daudi watched as his mother's hammer hit the big brown boulder.

A splinter broke off, and his mother frowned.

'Mama, you're tired,' he said. 'Let me do it.'

His mother looked up and smiled.

'Thank you, my son, but you are not strong enough.' She raised the hammer up high and brought it crashing down.

'I can do that Mama, I have muscles. See!'

His mother smiled when she saw the lump on Daudi's arm.

'Let me, please!' shouted Daudi.

'Hush!' cautioned his mother. 'You'll wake your sister!'

She had barely said this when the baby, lying nearby, began to cry. Daudi picked up the baby and carried her against his shoulder, patting her gently on the back.

'It's no use,' his mother sighed. 'I will just have to feed her!'

She sat against a rock and Daudi handed her the baby. Soon the noise of a baby sucking was all that could be heard in the afternoon heat.

Daudi looked at the little heap of stones where his mother had been working.

'Mama, what shall we do if no one buys our stones today?'

'We'll try again tomorrow,' his mother sighed.

'But we won't have money for food!'

'We still have a little from yesterday. Enough to buy some cassava.'

A tear rolled down Daudi's cheek.

'I'm hungry,' he whispered.

'Be brave, my child. We won't always break stones for food. One day I'll start sewing clothes again, and you won't go hungry any more.'

Daudi's eyes widened.

'I didn't know you could sew!'

'The landlord took away my sewing machine. We owed him a lot of money.'

'I will get you a new one tomorrow!' declared Daudi.

'You wish!' his mother laughed. Her breast slipped from the baby's mouth. The child had fallen asleep.

'We might as well go now,' she whispered. 'There are no buyers today.'

She tied her baby on her back and followed her son out of the stone quarry. They walked past some shops and stopped in front of the market, where heaps of cassava stood for sale.

'How was it today, Lillian?' the cassava-seller asked.

'It will be better tomorrow. Daudi's going to buy me a sewing machine!'

The cassava-seller looked at the small figure in front of her and shrieked with laughter.

'That Daudi! In his dreams, Lillian. In his dreams.'

When they reached home, Daudi left his mother resting with the baby on a mat. He ran to join his friends, who were watching a game of cards.

'Last card!' shouted a man in a blue cap, as he threw a card into the centre.

The other players shifted uneasily and Daudi clapped his hands in glee. His big friend Majid had slapped the winning card down.

'Ohhh!' the others groaned.

Majid turned to Daudi. 'How's it going my man?'

'Not bad. I want to buy my mother a sewing machine!'

The card-playing group went silent, then burst into laughter.

'Maybe he's won the lottery!' one of them winked.

'I know, he's found himself a winning bottle top!' another cheered.

'Stop teasing him!' Majid snapped. 'The boy just wants to help his mother. What's wrong with that?'

'Nothing!' a man wearing a green T-shirt answered. 'Except that he's dreaming.'

Majid shook his head.

'Not necessarily. A lot of people have won money from bottle tops.'

'Yes,' the man in the T-shirt jeered. 'But after drinking the soda. When has Daudi ever drunk soda, except for tasting what people leave at the bottom of their bottles?'

'I don't have to drink soda!' Daudi shouted. 'As long as I can get the bottle tops.'

Majid slapped his little friend on the back.

'That's the spirit. You get the bottle tops, and who knows what you may find inside?'

2 Daudi gets a job

Daudi ran down a row of shops until he came to some yellow umbrellas dotted outside a large doorway. The words 'Seiko's Café' were painted on them, in red. Under each umbrella was a table and chairs.

Bottle tops were scattered on the ground. Daudi looked to see who was watching, and quickly gathered them up into his shirt.

He hurried across the road and poured them out on to the pavement.

One by one, he pulled out the inside cover of each top and looked underneath it. He found nothing.

'I won't give up!' he muttered. He looked back across the road to where he had been.

A man and a woman were now sitting at one of the tables.
'If they order sodas,' thought Daudi, 'I will make sure I get their bottle tops.'

To Daudi's delight two bottles of soda were carried to the table. As soon as the waiter had removed the tops, Daudi nipped back across the road.

Before anyone could stop him, he swept his hand across the table top, grabbing the bottle tops.

'What was that?' the woman screamed.

'A street urchin, I think,' said her companion. 'What has he taken?'

'Our bottle tops!' was the astonished reply.

Daudi disappeared down an alley-way, and turned to see who was chasing him.

'No one's followed me!' he panted.

He stopped to catch his breath and opened his fist to look at his new bottle tops.

'This time!' he exclaimed smacking his lips. He slowly pulled off each cover – and found nothing.

Daudi's face fell.

'Let me go back,' he decided. 'There will be more customers by now, and more bottle tops.'

Daudi crept around the side of Seiko's Café. Many tables were now full of people, and drinks were being carried to and fro by sprightly waiters. Music was playing.

There were no bottle tops on the table nearest Daudi, but he could see one in the middle where several people had been sitting, and where there were a great many bottle tops.

Just then, a waiter, carrying a tray full of food and drinks, passed him. Daudi followed, hiding behind him, and stopped at the table where the bottle tops were.

'Hey!' the waiter shouted as Daudi snatched away the bottle tops.

He turned to run, and bumped the waiter's tray of food and drinks. The plates came tumbling down.

Daudi looked around wildly and tried to leap over the scattered mess.

'Gotcha!' a voice snarled as a hand grabbed his shoulder. A tall thin man with bony arms and a dark eye-patch across one eye dragged Daudi away from the tables and into the café.

'Don't hurt me!' Daudi pleaded. 'I was only looking for bottle tops!'

The hand dug into his shoulder and pulled him into a side room.

'Let him go, Evil Eye!' a deep voice said. 'He's not worth the trouble.'

Daudi looked up to see a man perched on a desk with one foot on the floor and the other swinging freely.

He wore a pink flowered shirt, a green sparkling waistcoat, and a cowboy hat. He carried a silver-topped walking stick.

'So you're the one who's been chasing around for bottle tops!' the man laughed. 'Well, if that's all you want, you can have them!'

Daudi fell on his knees and grabbed the man's shiny brown boot.

'Oh thank you, thank you sir,' he cried.

'There is one condition, however, that you start sweeping this café in exchange!'

'I will do anything!' Daudi whispered.

'Good. Start now!' the man ordered.

3 A lucky break

Daudi cleaned away the food and broken plates, and began sweeping under each table. He picked out the bottle tops from each pile of rubbish he swept up, and stuffed them inside his shirt.

'What's that noise?' a voice hissed in his ear, making poor Daudi jump.

'Wh... wh... what noise?'

'That rattling noise, whenever you move!' Evil Eye snapped.

'M...my b...bottle tops, y...you s...said I could have them.'

'But the rattling is disturbing my customers. GET RID OF THEM!' Evil Eye shouted.

'Wait a minute!' a familiar voice said. 'He's not disturbing us at all. You are the one shouting.'

Daudi looked up to see his friend Majid.

'Yes!' a woman dressed in red agreed. 'As the boy sweeps he rattles to the music. It's very entertaining. Let him be.'

Evil Eye scowled and stormed back inside the café.

Daudi picked up his broom and carried on sweeping, but this time it was a little different. He would lift a leg here, and shake his waist there, and the bottle tops jingled as he moved. Soon everyone was clapping and urging him on.

'Come on! ... Come on! ... Come on!' they cheered. Then, suddenly, the music stopped.

'Shame!' the people groaned.

'Never mind, sweeper boy,' the woman in red smiled. 'Here's 500 shillings for a soda.'

Daudi looked at the money in his hand. He thought about his mother and baby sister at home.

'Go on, spend it. I will replace it,' Majid whispered.

Daudi smiled and put his broom down. He ran inside the café, but stopped when he saw who was serving behind the counter.

'Get back to work!' Evil Eye growled.

'I've come to buy a soda,' Daudi mumbled.

'You! Where's the money?'

Daudi placed the money on the counter and Evil Eye looked at it and frowned. He opened a bottle of soda, and shoved it in the little boy's face.

'Can I have my bottle top?' Daudi whispered.

'Pick it up yourself.' Evil Eye snarled. He pointed at the bottle top, which had fallen on the floor.

Daudi looked around for a seat and saw one beside a fat little girl in a corner.

'My name's Sara, what's yours?' she asked when he sat down.

'Daudi,' he mumbled, as he concentrated on removing the cover from inside his bottle top.

Daudi's eyes nearly popped out as he looked, then looked again. Inside the bottle top was a bold black figure: 100,000/-.

'I've won!' he whispered. 'I've won the money for my Mama's sewing machine!'

'Let me see!' Sara shouted.

Before he could stop her, she had picked the bottle top from his open palm and was skipping with it around the room.

'Daudi has won!' she sang. 'One hundred thousand! Daudi has won!'

Evil Eye scrambled out from behind the counter.

'Let me see!' he shouted and snatched the bottle top from Sara's hand.

'Give that back!' Sara snapped.

Evil Eye handed her a bottle top.

'This is not the one you have just taken!' she shouted. 'This one has nothing on it!'

Daudi grabbed Evil Eye's shirt. 'Give me back my bottle top!' he wailed.

'She has it!' Evil Eye laughed as he pushed Daudi away.

'You liar!' Sara screamed. She looked around for someone to help her, but all the grown-ups were sitting outside. 'Give it back, or we'll report you!' Sara threatened.

'What's going on?' a deep voice asked. The three of them turned to face Mr Seiko.

'He's taken Daudi's winning top!' Sara cried.

'Oh please!' Mr Seiko laughed. 'Sweeper boy has no bottle tops here. They all belong to the café.'

'This one didn't, I bought the bottle of soda!' Daudi wailed.

'You bought a bottle of soda? With what money? Get out before I call the police!'

4 The bottle opener

Outside the café, Daudi and Sara walked around the tables.

'She's gone.' Daudi sighed. 'This is where the lady was sitting – the one who gave me the money.'

'Did anyone else see?' Sara asked.

'My big friend Majid, but he's gone too!'

Large drops of rain started to fall, and the people round the tables began to get up.

'Everyone's rushing inside,' Sara said. 'This is our chance!'

'For what?'

'To sneak back in without being seen, silly!'

Sara pulled Daudi to the café's entrance. 'Stay close behind me and we won't get caught.'

Sara and Daudi slipped into the café and hid behind the doors.

'What do we do now?' Daudi wondered.

'Look for your bottle top!'

Daudi's mouth dropped open.

'Among all these people?'

'No. It must be at the counter where Evil Eye works.'

The room was packed solid with people talking and laughing at the top of their voices. Music blared in the background.

The children got down on all fours and crawled between people's legs until they reached the counter.

'Phew!' Daudi gasped as they squeezed under the counter top among some crates. 'Where do you think he could have kept it?'

'I don't know. In an empty bottle perhaps.' Sara looked up at the counter over their heads.

'What's that?' she exclaimed.

A box-like shape was fixed underneath the counter top.

The children crawled towards it and examined it.

'It's a drawer, but it must be locked because I can't move it,' Daudi whispered.

Sara's face lit up.

'Evil Eye's bottle opener has a key on it! It might be the one for this drawer.'

'So how do we get a hold of his opener?' Daudi whispered.

Just then, footsteps approached the counter.

'Evil Eye, Seiko wants you!' a voice shouted over the music.

'OK, keep an eye on the drinks for me, it's a full house this evening.'

'I can't find my opener!' the voice said.

'Use mine, but don't lose it!'

The children heard an opener skid across the counter top as Evil Eye tossed it to the waiter.

They couldn't believe their ears when the waiter muttered, 'I can't make this one work. I'd better look for mine!'

Quick as a flash, Daudi nipped out from under the counter and snatched Evil Eye's opener. He and Sara rushed to the drawer and opened it.

Inside, they saw a khaki envelope.

'He's coming back!' Daudi whispered. Sara grabbed the envelope and pushed the drawer shut. She threw the key on to the counter and dived back into her hiding place behind Daudi.

Under the counter, Sara tipped the envelope open. Out fell a bottle top with the bold black figures of 100,000/- printed inside it.

'My bottle top!' Daudi gasped. 'Let's get out of here!'

Sara shook her head.

'What if Evil Eye returns now and decides to check his drawer? He will find his envelope missing and start looking for it.'

'So what are you saying?'

'We put it back before we leave.'

Daudi shrugged. Sara took another bottle top out of her pocket and slipped it inside the envelope.

'I'm returning the one he gave us!' she smiled.

The children waited for a chance to return the envelope. Their eyes followed the waiter's shoes as he served drinks at different points of the counter.

'Now!' Sara cried. The waiter had walked to the opposite end of the counter from the drawer. Daudi jumped out and popped the envelope inside the drawer. Moments later two small figures stepped out of the café doors.

5 The big day

'There's Sara!' Daudi shouted as he entered the factory gates. His mother was behind him, carrying the baby on her back.

'Is she the one who helped you yesterday?' his mother asked.

'Yes! Sara said she would meet us here for the prize-giving.' Daudi waved at Sara who came pushing through the crowd.

'I didn't realise there was going to be so many people,' she laughed. 'Do you think they have all won something?'

'No, most people have come to watch!' Daudi answered. 'This is my mother.' Sara bent her knees as she shook hands with Daudi's mother.

'Thank you for helping my son,' smiled Mama Daudi. The four of them entered the field in front of the soda factory and sat down on benches facing a large stage.

'Look! There's my big friend Majid!'

Daudi pointed at a rowdy group of men in the front row.

'And there's Evil Eye with Mr Seiko coming through the gates!' Sara shouted.

The children giggled as they watched Mr Seiko enter with a bounce as he twirled his stick and waved at Majid and his friends.

Evil Eye followed close behind him with his nose up in the air.

A man in a cap and T-shirt with the soda company's name on them walked up to the microphone on the stage.

'Please be seated everybody. The guest of honour is ready to give out the prizes.'

The noise quietened down as everyone turned to face the row of important looking people seated on stage.

'The first set of prize money is for those who found bottle tops with 20,000 shillings written inside them,' a woman announced.

A few people dotted around the benches stood up and were clapped and cheered as they showed their bottle tops to the announcer and were handed twenty thousand shillings each.

'The next prize money is for those who found bottle tops with 50,000 shillings written inside them,' announced the woman.

About four people stood up and a few others blew whistles as they claimed their prizes.

'Finally, we call forward any one who may have found the 100,000 shilling bottle top.'

Evil Eye jumped up in excitement and leapt on to the stage.

The crowd watched him pull out a khaki envelope and remove a bottle cap, which he showed to the announcer. The crowd gasped as the announcer shook her head.

Evil Eye snatched his cap back and looked at it.

'I don't believe it!' he screamed. 'I've been robbed!'

Factory guards came on to the stage to carry him off.

Daudi's mother quietly approached the stage.

'We have a winner!' The announcer declared.

People stood up and shouted, while others threw their caps in the air. A group of women started singing as Mama Daudi was handed her prize money.

Majid and his friends rushed on to the stage and lifted Mama Daudi on their shoulders.

'To the sewing machine shop!' she shouted as they carried her off.

At the shop, Mama Daudi handed the shopkeeper one hundred thousand shillings for a shiny black new sewing machine. They then proceeded home, past the front of the market where heaps of cassava stood for sale.

'How was it today, Lillian?' the cassava-seller asked.

'His dream came true Mary. My son's dream came true.'

The cassava-seller nearly fell off her seat as the sewing machine was carried past her.